This Journal Belongs to:

....

Shadow Work for Black Women

Strong, enduring, nurturing, self-sacrificing, the backbone of the community; getting up every day and donning the armor of the "strong black woman" is more than draining; it is damaging. The strong black woman is often expected to face injustice, racism, and disenfranchisement with a brave face, or ideally, "a smile." Standing steadfast in your persevering nature and strength to surmount these daily challenges is an unfortunate necessity, but doing so without self-compassion, personal truth, and emotional awareness can lead to physical, mental, emotional, and spiritual exhaustion.

Assuming the role of a mother, sister, bestie, spouse, and leader of your community necessitates a great degree of love and light. Yet, to deny your shadow self is to negate the pain and frustration caused by your trauma and, with it, the wisdom, learning, and growth that can be borne of it.

Your shadow self is not the "bad" part you need to get rid of. The shadow is only perceived as negative by those who fear it. The practice of shadow journaling enables you to accept and love all aspects of who you are, bringing repressed trauma and pain to the surface, creating opportunities for healing, understanding, growth, and ultimately change. While often triggering, shadow journaling is a profoundly transformative experience, as long as it is done from a place of vulnerability, self-love, and authenticity!

With shadow work, you will find yourself being compelled to confront a lot of dark things from your past. Things that you probably put away in mental boxes, sealed with duct tape, and kept hidden in the darkest corners of your mind. This can be very unpleasant, uncomfortable, and sometimes even draw up a well of pain that you've been trying to escape.

So how on earth could shadow work possibly be beneficial to you as a Black woman when it'll probably provoke a ton of tears and bring back unwanted memories?

Well, that's the thing about shadow work. The benefits lie in the challenges that it establishes. It's simply like an obstacle course. The wins lie at the end of the course. But you have to jump every hurdle, scale every wall, and crawl through every low to earn those wins.

In this journal, we will be taking an in-depth look, one by one, at all the benefits that healing through shadow work has to offer to the Black woman of today.

"The *shadow* is needed now more than ever.
We heal the world when we *heal ourselves*, and hope shines brightest when it *illuminates* the dark."

Sasha Graham

Shadow Work

There is a side to self-development and spirituality work that exists only in the deeper realms of our conscious and subconscious minds. The part of us who, for many, can feel like an unwanted houseguest overstaying their welcome, making us uncomfortable. This part of ourselves, the one that can be difficult to face, is our shadow. With everything in life there has to be balance and this, too, goes for us. The good, the bad, the light, the dark, the seen and the unseen. You may have heard about shadow work before, but in this journal, we will be breaking down exactly what it is, how the shadow self forms, how you can spot your inner shadow and, possibly most importantly, how you can make peace, and even learn to work with, your shadow self.

The Shadow Self

The birth of the shadow self.

We were all born pure, like blank canvases. But as we grow and develop from babies to infants, to teenagers and onwards, we learn knowledge that teaches us to separate things into good and evil. All throughout our lives since we were tiny infants we were distinctly taught what is "good" and what is "bad," what is "right" and what is "wrong," and what is "virtuous" and what is a "sin." Because of this, because of the beliefs we are taught so young, we feel we must try to deny the bad, to pretend it doesn't exist, for fear of being rejected or unloved by those in our lives.

It happens when your parents or caregivers may have told you to stop doing something, or reprimanded you for asking too many questions, or shouted at you for expressing yourself. When this happened, at a subconscious level, you decided that in order to keep your parents happy – and it's important to keep them happy as they are your only method of survival at this young age – you would bury this part of yourself, in essence hiding part of your authentic self. This is what becomes your shadow.

Yes, we all have a Shadow Self. As uncomfortable as it may sound, there is a dark side to every human being.

"But I'm a good person! I don't have a 'shadow' side," you might be thinking.

Well, the reality is that yes, you might be a good person.

In fact, you might be the most generous, loving, and selfless person in the entire world. You might feed the hungry, save puppies, and donate half of your salary to the poor. But that doesn't exclude you from having a Shadow. There are no exceptions here and it is nothing to be ashamed of.

Some people define the shadow self as the whole subconscious – anything that is not accessible to the conscious mind, whereas others define the shadow self as only those parts that our consciousness is unwilling to identify with – more so, that the ego will not identify with.

The nature of being human is to possess both a light and a dark side, and we need to embrace that. Sometimes, when people hear that they have a Shadow side (or when it is pointed out to them), there can be a lot of denial. We have been taught to perceive ourselves in a very two-dimensional and limited way. We have been taught that only criminals, murderers, and thieves have a Shadow side. This black-and-white thinking is one of the major causes of our suffering.

Without facing these thoughts and repressed desires within us, we increase the power of our Shadow Selves.

How to Spot the Shadow Self

The most powerful way you will likely spot the shadow in yourself is through other people. Others are your mirror – they reflect back to you the things you cannot, or will not, see in yourself and it is in these reflections where your shadows exist. Whenever you find yourself triggered by someone else's behavior, this is your shadow coming out. Remember, you cannot see in others what does not already exist in yourself, because if it weren't in you, you would be unable to recognize it.

Bitterness, jealousy, anger, resentment, hatred, guilt, shame, insecurity – these are all shadow emotions and if somebody triggers these feelings in you, it is because they are highlighting something within you that you feel is bad.

As well as this, you will notice your shadow self coming out when you find yourself projecting onto others your own thoughts, feelings or insecurities. Remember, everybody has their own version of reality and different people will find different things good, bad, funny, offensive, virtuous, self-centered...the list goes on. When you try to force your opinion, thoughts or feelings onto somebody else, this is your shadow side coming out and attempting to control people and situations. Notice, then, when you feel you might be trying to control what someone else is thinking or how they are feeling.

How to Start Accepting the Shadow Self

The first part of the process is acceptance of these thoughts, the ones that we have grown up thinking are 'bad'. As a result, a significant part of Shadow Work involves developing self-responsibility by accepting these thoughts. In the end, we must realize that there is nothing intrinsically "good" or "bad" about having such thoughts, and for us to move on with our lives, we must completely accept them.

Everything that irritates us about others can lead us to a better understanding of ourselves, everything we hear in our mind being said about ourselves is an opportunity to grow, every time we feel triggered by something we hear, read or see we are given the gift of learning. To start to accept the shadow self, starting to view it as a learning opportunity will open you up to a brand new way of thinking about yourself, others and the world.

Personal Growth and Self-Improvement

Shadow work is crucial to your self-growth and self-improvement.

Growth is all about stepping out of the old and into the new and the better. However, it might be impossible to discover the new and better you if you don't know who you are right now as well as who you've been in the past.

If you do not confront the parts of yourself that you've hidden (for any reason at all), those "shadows" will always come back to haunt you. They may even cause you to remain stagnant, unable to encounter your future because your past is holding you back. Your shadows can cause you self-doubt, make you scared to go for what you want, mentally enslave you and make you underproductive, and generally hinder you from becoming your best self.

Thus, the intervention of shadow work will enable you to break through all these barriers to your self-growth and self-improvement. Self-improvement for Black women is so important, especially today. We're now able to reach for heights that we could've only dreamed of attaining in the past. High-quality education. Jobs that we couldn't get hired into before owing to racism and sexism. Political positions. Winning prestigious awards and honorable recognitions. Inventing and innovating ideas and technology that revolutionize the world.

There's so much that we Black women are capable of in the society of today. Therefore, to realize our greatness, we must weaken the hold that our shadows have on us. And this is where shadow work can help.

Healing Journey

Shadow work starts you off properly on your healing journey.

When you've experienced deep pain and hurt—whether physical, mental, or emotional—you often get different therapies and rehabilitation methods recommended to you. Most of these therapies thrust you right into how to move on and look into a brighter future. Unfortunately, that's not the best way to begin healing.

To effectively heal from anything—could be trauma, rejection, depression, a broken heart, disappointment, grief, or failure—you must begin by addressing your pain. It has been statistically proven that Black women experience more trauma at a disproportionate rate to other individuals, particularly traumas that are related to sex, reproduction, and grief from losing loved ones. So in order to begin true healing, you must confront and acknowledge these traumas first.

I'd also like to state that whatever you may have been through or experienced in life, you're not a victim. You're a survivor. So as you reacquaint yourself with your pain and your "shadows" and begin your journey towards healing, you should keep in mind that those shadows don't completely define you. Once you begin to experience genuine healing, you will discover all over again how strong you really are as a Black woman.

A special aspect of this benefit is the part that has to do with healing from generational trauma. This has to do with healing from very early wounds, often inflicted or caused by primary caregivers like a parent. This is especially important so that the lineage of generational trauma can end with you and you don't end up passing it on to your own children.

Authenticity

Shadow work breeds authenticity.

Shadow work forces you to confront the real you, not just the you that the world finds acceptable.

As you know, your "shadows" are the sides of yourself that hold your repressed traumas, humiliations, guilts, and all the parts of yourself that you've sought to hide not just from others but also from yourself. Shadow work brings these shadows to light, and by doing this, stops you from being in denial of who you truly are.

Again, your shadows don't completely define you. They may be truths about your life and your past, but they're not what makes you authentic. What makes you authentic is the fact that you're a woman who has faced her fears, faced her pain, and discovered how strong and truly better she can become for it.

Shadow work makes you own up to your past and build a brighter future for yourself on a foundation of self-awareness and authenticity.

Strength

Shadow work reaffirms your strength.

Shadow work, when done right, is never easy. And so being able to go successfully undergo this therapy will prove to you all over again that there's really nothing that you cannot conquer as a Black woman. This will build up your confidence, self-esteem, and all-round belief in yourself.

" The shadow is made up of all of the parts of ourselves that we have to deny hard in order to *fit into our culture."*

Feel Whole

Shadow work makes you feel whole.

Having an unpleasant part of yourself that you keep in the shadows can make you feel broken at times. It's not only about the pain and the hurt. It also has to do with the knowledge that there's a part of you that you may be ashamed or unwilling to admit to or acknowledge.

Shadow work will help you to understand that despite the feelings of disjointedness and disadvantage that your life's experiences may elicit, not only can you become whole but you have really always been whole. There's nothing broken or damaged about you, irrespective of your past or present. And even if you carry scars from your past, you're are still such a bold and beautiful woman. Shadow work will help you see this clearly.

Relationships

Shadow work helps with how you interact with others.

As your self-awareness heightens through shadow work, you'll learn to trust yourself more. And that trust will extend into improving your relationships.

This is based on the premise that you can't love others if you do not love yourself. Through shadow work, you will come to love and accept every single facet of your being. And by this, your ability to love and respect others, and even validate the struggles of those who have also experienced their own share of pain and hurt in the past will be strengthened.

You will also become better at standing up for yourself. Your heightened self-love will lead to an increased dedication to your self-care. This will embolden you to develop your boundaries and enforce them whenever it comes to your relationships and interactions with others.

Healthier Habits

Shadow work helps you to develop healthier habits.

Your shadow self will often lead you to develop destructive behaviors such as putting yourself down, procrastination, body dysmorphia, addiction, stress eating, and more. You might even begin to justify some of these behaviors as your "coping mechanisms". If not curbed, these behaviors can prove to be ruinous and even fatal to your wellbeing.

Shadow work can help you to nip these behaviors at the bud —the bud being your shadow self. After confronting the reasons for these behaviors, shadow work will then shift your focus to finding healthier and more constructive habits to replace the destructive ones. When you become honest with and open to every aspect of yourself, it becomes a lot easier to be in control of your habits. This way, you can crush the bad ones and substitute them with better ones.

Overall Wellness

Shadow work will improve your overall wellness.

Suppressing your shadow self can result in all sorts of problems. You may not even realize these problems stem from a repressed side of yourself until you begin to confront that side.

Shadow work will put the control of your wellness back into your hands. The therapy will start at the root causes to address every problem you may be experiencing. It won't just treat your anxiety, chronic fatigue, or any other problem on the surface. It will tackle them from their origins.

Conclusion

Shadow work enables you to discover and accept the authentic you. As a Black woman, this is extremely important because many of us have struggled for long with our identities. Shadow work therapy will help you to prevail against that struggle. Accepting your identity fully not only improves your own wellness and mental health but also makes you open to accepting others for who they are as well. Finally, the practice of shadow work may not be easy, but the ends make it totally worth it.

Let's begin

working

with your shadow!

A vow to myself...

I..,

vow to accept myself, to love all of my flaws, and to put myself and my *healing* first.

I vow to let myself *feel my emotions.*

I choose to *embrace my wounds.*

I deserve the world and even a little more.

Today and for the rest of my days, I choose to *love* myself, *cherish* myself, and to *accept* myself, just the way that I am.

I look forward to unveiling my shadows.

....

How do you feel about your childhood?
Was it generally positive or negative?

Outline the most prominent memories that
you have of your younger years.

_____
_____
_____
_____
_____
_____
_____
_____
_____
_____
_____
_____
_____
_____
_____
_____
_____
_____
_____
_____
_____
_____
_____
_____
_____

What's your worst childhood memory?

What could have made your childhood better?
How do you feel about that?

What was life like growing up as a Black child?
Would you describe your childhood as happy?

Have you ever experienced racial discrimination?
Describe your experience.

As a Black woman, what are some challenges you face
because of the color of your skin?
List some subtle signs of discrimination.

Recall the first time you experienced racism as a child. How did it make you feel?

Does this experience still affect you as an adult?
In what ways?

Do you have any other traumatic childhood memories?

Are you comfortable in your skin?
If there is something that you would like to change
about yourself, what is it and why?

Growing up, were there non-black traits or
features that you wish you had?
Do you still wish you had these traits?

_____

_____

_____

_____

_____

_____

_____

_____

_____

_____

_____

_____

_____

_____

_____

_____

_____

_____

_____

_____

_____

Which of your Afrocentric features do you have a difficult time celebrating?

What's the worst character trait you have as a result of your childhood? What or who do you think caused it?

What is your relationship like with your family?
Has your connection strengthened since you were
a child or has it gotten worse?

What are your parent's or guardian's best and
worst personality traits?
Do you see any of them within yourself?

_____
_____
_____
_____
_____
_____
_____
_____
_____
_____
_____
_____
_____
_____
_____
_____
_____
_____
_____
_____
_____
_____
_____
_____
_____
_____
_____

What role do you feel your parents or guardians played in defining failure or success when you were a child?

*Do you feel your parents or guardians set different standards
for you as a Black girl /woman?*

What were some beliefs your parents or guardians held about race when you were growing up? Which were helpful? Which were harmful?

Do you share your parent's or guardian's beliefs about race? Why or why not?

How do you handle the stress of daily living?

What are some words you would use to describe yourself?

List 10 things you love about yourself.

Do you think being a Black woman has any effect on hindering you from living life to your highest potential? Why or why not?

_____

_____

_____

_____

_____

_____

_____

_____

_____

_____

_____

_____

_____

_____

_____

_____

_____

_____

_____

Make a list of the forms of discrimination Black women face daily on a large scale.

Are you happy with where you are in your life?

What in your life gives you the most purpose?

How did you deal with trauma in the past and what
do you do to combat it in the present?

What things are triggers for you?
Consider where those feelings stem from.

Do you have any unhealthy attachments or habits?
What are you doing to curb them and why have you
continued to entertain them?

Do you accept yourself as you are?

What makes you feel most valued?

Do you practice self-care?
Is there more that you could be doing for your wellbeing?

_____

_____

_____

_____

_____

_____

_____

_____

_____

_____

_____

_____

_____

_____

_____

_____

_____

_____

_____

_____

_____

_____

_____

_____

_____

Write about a thing that's happened to you that has made you a stronger person.

What is one piece of advice you would give someone who has gone through the same situation?

*How do you reassure yourself of how proud
you are to be a woman of color?*

Do you tend to judge yourself?
What do you judge yourself for?

What situations make you feel not good enough?
In what ways are these triggers of unworthiness
influenced by race?

What emotions do you tend to avoid?

What are some ways you could be more
patient with yourself?

What are your core values? Why have you chosen them? How do you live your values on a daily basis?

When do you feel the most confidence in yourself?

_____

_____

_____

_____

_____

_____

_____

_____

_____

_____

_____

_____

_____

_____

_____

_____

_____

_____

_____

_____

_____

_____

What practices do you carry out to feel your best?

Make a list of ten self-acceptance affirmations.

How deserving do you truly believe you are?

Is there anyone in your life that you are competitive with? If yes, what caused this rivalry?

Have you ever found yourself in a position where you had to struggle to maintain your identity as a Black woman? Describe the situation.

_____
_____
_____
_____
_____
_____
_____
_____
_____
_____
_____
_____
_____
_____
_____
_____
_____
_____
_____
_____
_____
_____
_____
_____
_____
_____

Have you ever experienced microaggression?
Write about what happened.

Have you ever been looked down on because of your race or gender? Write what happened.
What was your reaction to the situation?

What is something you love but hide from your non-black
peers for fear of being judged as
"ghetto" or "hood"?

What is something you love but hide from your black peers
for fear of being judged as
"white-washed" or "bougie."

If you could change one thing about the world,
what would it be?

What do you think are the worst character traits a person can have?
When is a time you have demonstrated these traits?

When is the last time you felt let down?
Examine how you felt and whether it was truly rational,
or if you were triggered.

_____

_____

_____

_____

_____

_____

_____

_____

_____

_____

_____

_____

_____

_____

_____

_____

_____

_____

_____

_____

_____

_____

What do you dislike about yourself most?

How do you think people see you?
How would they describe you? How do you feel about that?

Do you feel misunderstood?
If yes, what misconceptions do people have of you?

What misconceptions do you feel non-black people have about you?

Have you found yourself going to great lengths to disprove these misconceptions? If so, how does that make you feel?

What is the biggest lie you believe or used to believe about yourself as a Black woman?

_____
_____
_____
_____
_____
_____
_____
_____
_____
_____
_____
_____
_____
_____
_____
_____
_____
_____
_____
_____
_____
_____
_____
_____

What is something you would tell your younger self if you could?

What influence do you feel your race has on your religious or spiritual beliefs? Is this influence harmful or helpful?

What is something that happened in your life that made you feel weak?

How do you react when you are happy, excited, frustrated, or sad in the company of non-black individuals?

How do you react when you are happy, excited, frustrated, or sad in the company of black individuals?

Does your emotional expression differ across circumstances?
If so, how? Why do you think that is?
How does that make you feel?

How do you feel about confronting a non-black person who has wronged you?

_____

_____

_____

_____

_____

_____

_____

_____

_____

_____

_____

_____

_____

_____

_____

_____

_____

_____

_____

_____

_____

_____

_____

_____

_____

_____

How do you feel about confronting a black peer
who has wronged you?

_____

_____

_____

_____

_____

_____

_____

_____

_____

_____

_____

_____

_____

_____

_____

_____

_____

_____

_____

_____

_____

_____

_____

Does your self-expression differ across circumstances?
If so, How? Why do you think that is?
How does that make you feel?

*Do you ever find yourself overthinking how you've expressed
yourself or behaved in social settings?
Do you feel race triggers these social anxieties? If so, how?*

Are you 100% yourself around others? Do you put on a persona or mask to blend into the crowd? Do you know who you are?

_____
_____
_____
_____
_____
_____
_____
_____
_____
_____
_____
_____
_____
_____
_____
_____
_____
_____
_____
_____
_____
_____
_____
_____

Do you enforce boundaries with others or
are you the type to let people cross lines?

Do you respond well to constructive criticism?
Are you over-sensitive to any form of feedback?

Have you ever discussed issues of racial inequality
with non-black people?
If so, what were your experiences like?

What were the positive takeaways of discussing inequality with non-black people, if any?
What were the negative takeaways, if any?

Do you feel as though people respect you?

How do you feel when you see acts of aggression or brutality
against black people in the media?
How do you cope with these feelings?

_____
_____
_____
_____
_____
_____
_____
_____
_____
_____
_____
_____
_____
_____
_____
_____
_____
_____
_____
_____
_____
_____
_____
_____
_____

What are some toxic traits you have and how does it affect others?

How do these traits impact your daily life as a Black woman?

_____
_____
_____
_____
_____
_____
_____
_____
_____
_____
_____
_____
_____
_____
_____
_____
_____
_____
_____
_____
_____
_____
_____
_____

How does the weight of the generational trauma of being a Black woman make you feel?

How does your unique trauma as a Black woman
make you feel?

How do you cope with both types of trauma?

Which coping mechanisms are healing,
which are hurtful, if any?

Is it easy for you to ask for help? Does it make you feel weak or vulnerable? Why do you think this is?

When have you been self-sabotaging or destructive in your life? Examine how you were feeling at the time, and what triggered your behavior.

What is your deepest, darkest fear?

*How might you be able to expose yourself
to that fear in a safe way?*

Do you lie to yourself to avoid addressing your fears?

What is something you wish you could share about your experience as a Black woman with non-black people as a whole?

_____

_____

_____

_____

_____

_____

_____

_____

_____

_____

_____

_____

_____

_____

_____

_____

_____

_____

_____

_____

_____

_____

_____

What are some social issues and problems you believe Black women face in the world?

Propose some well-thought-out solutions to these problems.

What is one question you had about race as a child that you never feel you got an honest answer to?

Write about a time you experienced something that seemed negative but turned out to be a positive thing in the long run.

What is your biggest regret and why?

What memories bring you shame?
Think about who you were then, what led to your behavior,
and how you've changed since.
Now write out the words 'I forgive myself".

*Do you forgive yourself when you have done something
wrong? When you make mistakes can you move on from
them or do they continue to hurt you?*

Are you happy to be alone in your own company?
Do you use other people to fill a void?

Who has the most influence over you?
Is that healthy?

Who regularly belittles or downplays your emotions? How does it make you feel?

What is your relationship to drama? Do you like it?
Involve yourself in it? Cause it? Explore this.

How do you handle stress? What are some things you can do to care for yourself during stressful times?

Who do you envy? Why?
How might you be able to work towards gaining the things
they have that you feel jealousy towards?

Who are you closest to in your life and do they positively reflect who you are? Are you holding on to people that don't deserve your time and affections? Are you honestly happy in your relationships?

What kind of people do you surround yourself with?

How do they help you in reassuring yourself of your worth?

Was there a time you opened yourself up to someone and felt rejected? What happened? How has that affected you?

Do you allow yourself to be vulnerable in your romantic relationships? Do you put up walls around yourself and your partner or are you completely open?

_____

_____

_____

_____

_____

_____

_____

_____

_____

_____

_____

_____

_____

_____

_____

_____

_____

_____

_____

_____

_____

_____

_____

_____

_____

What makes you jealous? Why do you think these people or circumstances make you feel that way?

What does it tell you about your own needs?
Are these things you can work towards or something
you should let go of?

Have you ever been in a codependent relationship? What about your family members? Talk about your experience with codependency as well as thoughts or feelings that come up about it.

Think of a relationship you've walked away from.
Write down the reasons it's been a positive life choice.

Think about your friendships. Which ones make you feel safe, secure, and loved? Do you have any in which you feel isolated, pressured, or uncomfortable?

Is there anyone you hold a grudge against? If so, what is holding you back from letting go and moving on?

Who is someone that annoys you?
How can you show them kindness and compassion?

What person has hurt you the most in your life?

Which relationships in your life no longer serve you?
Which relationships feel obligatory or dutiful?

Consider how you'd feel if you allowed those relationships to dissolve, then think about whether they're worth trying to salvage, and how you may be able to do that.

How have your challenges in life helped you with self-discovery?

What is a recent lesson you have learned?

How are you letting yourself down at this time in your life?
How could you be better to yourself?
Consider your health, finances, relationships, work, etc.

Where do you derive your sense of self-worth from?
Is this a healthy or unhealthy source?

*The way you spend your time daily will determine
how you spend the rest of your life.
What are your thoughts on this?*

Pick a core limiting belief that you have and write it down.
Why do you think this belief is true about you?

When was the last time you forgave yourself completely?
How did that feel?

For some reason, have you neglected your mental health?
Why?

What do you need to stop avoiding?

What version of yourself do you try to portray to the world?
Are you being your authentic self?

What are 5 things you are always grateful for?

What would you most like to be recognized for?

What answer do you have for your inner child now?

Shadow Work
Activities and Exercises

Activity #1

Others are my mirror.

What we see in others has to exist in ourselves, otherwise we would be unable to recognize it. So, have a think about a person, or group of people, that irritate, anger or annoy you, or perhaps make you feel jealous or 'less than'. Think about what it is specifically that makes you feel this way – what is it they do, how do they act, what words do they use that trigger this response in you?

Be totally truthful here, there's no-one other than you who will see this. What do you dislike about them? If you could say this to them, what would you say?

And then, have a conversation with this part within yourself – the part you wouldn't usually allow to have a voice.

So, if you feel anger towards them, lean into this feeling within yourself and ask it:

'What are you trying to show me?'

Why are you here?

What are you keeping me safe from?

What are you trying to teach me?

Where did you come from?

By doing this and by giving this shadow part of yourself a voice, you'll be able to dig into where the feeling has come from and, eventually, pinpoint it back to a similar feeling you will have had as a child.

....

....

....

....

....

....

....

....

....

....

....

....

....

....

Activity #2

End of day reflection.

Reflection of any sort is always an incredible tool to help with personal development, and in this case it can really help with shadow work. At the end of each day take 5-10 minutes to reflect on anyone who has triggered any feelings in you that don't feel good – anger, upset, frustration, jealousy, sadness. Take a few minutes to think about what they were doing or saying when you felt the shadow self arise, and where your thought process went.

If it's helpful to carry a journal and pen around with you, you can do this reflection as soon as you have recognized a sensation that you believe to be from the shadow self.

What triggered these feelings and where in your own life do you think these traits have shown up?

....

....

....

....

....

....

....

....

....

....

....

Activity #2

Good vs. Bad

Challenge the good parts of you. We are always praised for being a 'good girl' or 'good boy', and so we cling on to these parts of ourselves and try hard to disregard anything that differs from this. This is what then becomes the shadow – the part that isn't deemed good or worthy.

So, for this exercise, write down all of the things that make you a good person, and then write down the exact opposite. Understand, accept and embrace that all aspects of these are within you and they all combine to make you who you are. Remember, when you reject a part of yourself– as we so often reject the shadow side – you are effectively denying the ability you have to be your whole authentic self.

....

....

....

....

....

....

....

....

....

....

....

....

Activity #4

Create an open dialogue.

Have a conversation with someone who triggers your shadow side, if appropriate. It's not always going to be possible, and it will certainly feel uncomfortable, but if you can and the person is willing, have an open dialogue with the person and make it clear to them that you are not trying to offend or hurt them in any way, but that you are simply trying to understand yourself better. Of course, this won't necessarily work with a distant work colleague or someone you know little about, but if it is someone who you trust and have a relatively open relationship with, then you can give it a go.

The best way to do this is to ask them about themselves and learn more about them first, because you will likely find that the negative thoughts you had about them – perhaps that they're conceited, a goody-two-shoes or arrogant – will likely be dispersed once you get to know them a little more. We often make up stories and beliefs in our mind about people because the brain likes to fill in the blanks of missing information, so always take your first impressions of people with a pinch of salt.

As already mentioned, it's likely that your brain has made up the negative traits of a person because of your beliefs and experiences, so getting to know the real person will help to train your brain to recognize that not everything it thinks is actually the truth.

Activity #5

The Overachiever.

This exercise involves thinking about the areas in life where you tend to overdo things. This can be so-called good or bad areas where you overdo things and the below list, while not comprehensive will help to identify such possible areas:

+ Overworking,

+ Over-eating,

+ Over-pleasing,

+ Over-apologizing,

+ Over-compromising,

+ Over-fussing,

+ Over-restricting,

+ Over-indulging (not necessarily just with food, but with shopping, alcohol etc.).

This will show not only what you feel you value in life, which has impacts on other areas, but also how you engage with yourself and others. Are you giving yourself enough time for self-care, for example? If you feel triggered when you see other people doing self-care, perhaps thinking things like 'They're lazy and overindulgent', then this is highly likely because you are repressing a part of yourself, one that was called lazy when you were younger (remember, it doesn't have to have only been verbal, it could have been a look or a gesture that insinuated this).

Forgiveness Letter

Forgiveness is such a healthy act. Especially at times when a conflict occurs between you and someone else, forgiveness is the only way to expel the negative energy of malice and replace it with a healthier and more positive vibe. It's the only key to moving on from past wrongs.

For many of us, it can be really hard to forgive, especially when the other person has deeply hurt us. But the truth is that once you master the art of forgiveness, you'll be able to maintain fuller control over your emotions and your life in general.

One thing you need to realize, however, is that holding grudges and refusing to forgive someone can be counterproductive because it acts as emotional baggage that holds you down and impedes your progress. It's easy to see grudges as your way of making the other person feel bad. But actually, you are hurting yourself.

Writing them a forgiveness letter sets you free and helps you find that inner peace. Before you write the letter, you want to reflect on everything that happened between you and this person. You want to think of what led to the conflict and also the role you played. Write to them letting them know you have forgiven them. In the letter, you might also want to talk about what you could have done differently. Don't forget the goal of this letter is to set get rid of the emotional baggage holding you back. After writing your letter, you don't have to send it to them. The goal is for you to find inner peace, and you've done the hard work, which is pouring out your emotions into writing.

How writing a forgiveness letter works

We've established that forgiveness relieves you of any emotional burden and fully places the control over your life back in your hands. When writing a forgiveness letter, the main purpose is for you to find inner peace. Therefore, you don't essentially have to send the letter to the other person—unless you feel like sending it would benefit you.

Hence, because the letter is fully for your benefit, feel free to express your emotions completely and openly, then articulate your forgiveness at the end.

How to write a forgiveness letter

1. Begin by considering the opposite perspective:

Recall your relationship with the person before the conflict. Did you have a good relationship with them? Did you love them? How did you feel during the conflict and afterward?

Think about how the other person must've felt during the conflict as well. Try and empathize with them if possible—you may be able to achieve this by reminding yourself that they're human too and we all make mistakes. Could there have been something going on in their life that made them act that way? Were they probably acting out their insecurities or fears?

2. Simulate forgiveness:

Imagine yourself granting the person forgiveness. What are the emotions that surface as you imagine this? What does your facial expression look like? Which physical sensations arise in your body?

Try to tangibly feel all the sensations from your imagination, regardless of whether it feels like you're faking it. This will actually serve as a sort of practice stage before the real forgiveness.

3. Write the forgiveness letter:

Following the imagination or practice stage, sit down and write a forgiveness letter to the person.

+ Describe in detail how the person wronged or hurt you.

+ Explain how their actions affected you at the time and if you still feel hurt by those actions.

+ State what you wish the other person had done instead—the exercise of empathizing with the other person will assist you in this part.

+ End the letter with a clear statement of forgiveness and understanding. For example, "I understand that you may have said what you did coming from a place of concern so I'm choosing to let it go, forgive you and move on."

Remember that it's totally up to you to choose whether to send the letter or not. The entire exercise is for your full benefit so do what you feel will be in your best interest.

Forgiveness Letter

Forgiveness Letter

Forgiveness Letter

Notes & Reflections

Notes & Reflections

Notes & Reflections

Notes & Reflections

Also available from
Limitless Abundance

That's all for now!

We would love to hear from you!
Your opinion matters to us!
Share with us your transformation success stories and how
this journal is helping you –
it will create a positive change and inspire others!

If you enjoyed this journal,
please don't forget to leave a review on Amazon.

Just a simple review helps us a lot!

Thank you,

Limitless Abundance

Printed in Great Britain
by Amazon

22221576R00096